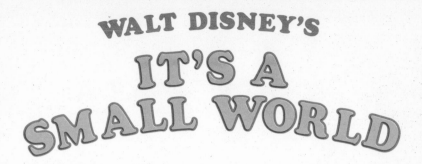

WALT DISNEY'S
IT'S A SMALL WORLD

A Golden Book • New York
Western Publishing Company, Inc., Racine, Wisconsin 53404

Once there was a little orphan boy who did not know his real name. He didn't even know which country he came from. He was called Bobby at the children's home where he stayed.

One day he went on a trip to Disneyland with the
other children. He sat all by himself on the bus.
"I wish I belonged to a country," he thought.

When the bus reached Disneyland, everyone went through the gates. Bobby became separated from the other children. He looked up and saw a beautiful palace with an enormous white and gold clock in front.

It was the biggest clock Bobby had ever seen.
He got into a boat to take a closer look. As the boat
sailed past the clock face, the chimes rang the hour.

Suddenly Bobby was in an enchanted place. The signs said "welcome" in many languages. A group of Scandinavian children sang to him, while ice skaters whirled about on a rink above the water.

A little farther on, the boat reached the British Isles. Wee folk were playing on a beautiful Irish harp. "Maybe I'm Irish," said Bobby, hopefully.

Then he heard English children singing to him from London Bridge and a little Scottish piper playing his bagpipes.

A flock of geese joined in the melody in Belgium,
and in Holland boys and girls, seated on tulips,
clicked their wooden shoes in time to the music.

When Bobby arrived in Spain and Portugal,
children were playing and dancing.
    "It's time we're aware,
        There's so much that we share," they sang.

When he reached Italy, future opera stars were
singing arias by the leaning tower of Pisa. In France
graceful Parisian dancers were putting on a show.
An Alpine yodeler's voice rang out to the
accompaniment of Swiss bells.

In Russia a row of Cossacks danced to a balalaika band.

The sky in the Middle East was filled with magic
flying carpets. "What fun it would be to ride on
one!" said Bobby.

A little Greek shepherd boy played on his pipes of Pan. "Why, they're all playing the same song!" thought Bobby.

There was a wonderful Indian snake-charmer.

A golden goddess reigned over the land of Bali.

Japanese boys were flying dragon kites
above an orange Torii gate.

And in Africa, there were wonderful animals! Hippos, monkeys, giraffes, and a laughing hyena. "Maybe I came from Africa," Bobby thought.

There was an Egyptian boy on his very own camel!

In South America everyone was dancing.
Bobby wanted to dance with them.

He came to the end of the voyage with the words of the song running through his mind. "Just one moon, and one golden sun." And "A smile means friendship to everyone...it's a small, small world."

He still did not know which country he came from, but he knew that a part of him belonged to every country. And a part of every country belonged to him!

"it's a small w

The boat sailed out into the bright sunlight and
stopped. Bobby got out. He saw the boys and girls
from the children's home and ran to join them.

He no longer felt alone. He had
friends all over the world!
"It's a Small World"...after all!